STILL
I AM PUSHING

poems by

Candice M. Kelsey

Finishing Line Press
Georgetown, Kentucky

STILL
I AM PUSHING

ACKNOWLEDGMENTS

Publisher: Leah Maines
Editor: Christen Kincaid
Cover Art: Tracy Neilson
Author Photo: Leora Lorraine Wright
Cover Design: Heather Holmes

Printed in the USA on acid-free paper.
Order online: www.finishinglinepress.com
       also available on amazon.com

Author inquiries and mail orders:
Finishing Line Press
P. O. Box 1626
Georgetown, Kentucky 40324
U. S. A.

Table of Contents

for my daughters
Georgia Rae & Israel Marlene

and for my son
Michael David

Prologue:

"The ways in which
I am
my mother's daughter
are infinite."

~ Roxane Gay, *Hunger*

Still I am Pushing

For many years, a white coat was a death sentence for a boxer puppy,
and breeders routinely drowned their white puppies.

Snow tubing
this winter's day
San Bernardino National Forest
clouds and pine
combine
high elevation calico
called Snow Drift
hills like
white boxer puppies
a sun like Sol Invictus
at St. Peter's

my son's nose
cold and red
a tiny Japanese flag
perfect drop of blood
on a white sheet
mocking compass in the corner
of a map
Chinese flag
with its gold star
like a mother
whose four little stars
fan out to nurse
each nipple a pennant
crimson

Red as that call button
on the wall
by my parents' bed
for an emergency
the police
call button I should have
pushed

the moment I knew
what my mother knew
all along—
white puppies
will be drowned

Because always
even now
I push I *push* and still
I am pushing
my finger
even as I speed down a hill
snow tubing
over patterned continents
white pages
like bruised ice
sudden hematoma
of memory
forty years later
I listen
for sirens that never come.

Parode:

My mother let me shower with her
I had been begging
Unforgettable the weight of water
I never asked again

Small Places I've Filled

My mother's womb
the playhouse
born of my father's hands
laundry chute
and linen closet
back seat of a Corolla
that tiny studio
Chicago.
A boy's heart.

I climb into these
spaces frantic
a wild boar hunted
trembling.
I sniff
get comfortable—

I climb into
these poems
whose words linger
like lint
from a motel-quilt
sky. Yet

always
there's pleasure
settling my body
home
where I can
pull the curtains
burn incense
and fill
pages
like bodies do coffins.

She Calls

In other rooms of years ago
        She sometimes calls to me
This small girl dancing on tip-toe—
        The child I used to be.

And how she beams so beautifully
        Once she has climbed within
I think perhaps she wants to be
        The woman I could have been.

Strophe:

A turning of the feet
a hasty wheel—
And all at once
the heart is shot to smithereens

Gunkholing

This September night at home
on my flats-boat bed
whose low rumbling motor
I've turned off,
my children and their guests
slumber between the reeds.

I am no longer a sleepy woman
but the guide standing aft
slowly maneuvering
this hunk of aluminum
through shallow tidal water,
cold stiff pole in my hands.

I can take it through bogs,
shadow-strewn and teeming
like imagination,
this silent floating body
is the pulse of my own flesh
shut down to a slow surge
just enough to stay afloat,
so beautifully numb.
I ascend the raised platform.

Detached entirely I ignore
my spittle on the pillow
and see the waters
ripple and gurgle and glide,
the boat jerk and yield.

But if I'm not in my body,
if I'm just the detached guide
when he forces his hands,
his mouth, why do I still feel
the quick cool breath
of the ceiling's oars on my face
like the spray of shoal water
from a fisherman's cruel heave?

Fearless Girl

installed on March 7, 2017, in the Financial District of Manhattan

Rendered from
cellulose & hydrocarbons
lightweight
polymers molded. Extruded. Cast
re-cast & blown product
of the Nobel Prize (Chemistry)

liquid resins squeezed through spinnerets.
Monitor. Adjust
machines little more than crossword clues
this jargon / pliable diction
overlooked & forgotten

like the countless careful
hands & minds
of Mesopotamia:
ancient Egyptians. Canaanites. Hebrews.
Phoenicians—

like the alphabet of a girl
(tiny wedge)
who is never heard
who is 250 pounds of bronze
who is 50 inches
of gender-diverse senior leadership (SSgA)

corporate feminism. MAGA. Di Modica
and Pissing Pug:
melting snow. America

she makes a difference
at the intersection of Broadway & Whitehall
on the NASDAQ
before the bull—
        all the bulls

Anti-Strophe:

Each spring brother's baseball
A distraction: I could slip into her
Wedding gown twirl on the back porch
(Budding trees gave blessings)

Daughter's Lament

I am just a blue print
across the drafting table
under
your heavy stone
palms pressing
my corners

Your red pencil
a sundial
to cast shadows
on my body
this body is paper

Not daughter but design—

A shade
Turn-bell and Prussian
blue dayflower
petals
tiny cradles

these lines
my mask
careful measurements
my song

Negatives
of the original
ultraviolet light
mother
and father

I am not
easily altered
the scales unreliable
skin at times
brittle

ink soaked once
the excess
has washed away

I see
what you want to erect

That wrought iron vane
appearing
through the bay window
plate glass
terrible steel sash

The brick corbels set
on the right
to hide wooden lintels
breathing
the tower's cornice

But you
must suit your lot
improve aesthetics
birth lean
symmetry
reduce this thigh
lengthen then pull
or push
to add more here

Elbow the workers
to look
my sashay of hips
you taught me
offer hips
one night I paid for it
met the morning
bruised

Unlike my attackers
gently
roll me up
swaddle me thick
rubber band
cylinder coffin-click
when your pencil
is dull

Stand in the mirror
unroll your
own face
take a favorite lipstick
and slash.

Toward an Arctic Circle

There are lines
my mother and I
cross borders
we step past

where flesh and bone
meet cranberry
and clubmoss
outside the truth
I like to call
our lower forty-eight.

We paddle
sometimes motor
up the Wild
Salmon River
toward the Boreal
Forest I know
as the northern limits
of mother and
daughter.

Like today
when she texted
I'm watching Dr. Phil
between caribou
and birch
and now I realize
I involved you
in adult issues when
you were just
a teen forgive me
Candice.

I mark time
to the rhythm of
the Great Kobuk dunes

while she inhales
the onion portage its
naked chive
growth glowing like
the screen
of my phone.

I'm watching
the white ruffs
chalk caribou
bulls' noble antlers
I read their
autumn pelage verse
and succumb to
my marrowed guilt

for hesitating
to accept this apology
not because
she's thirty years late
to this continual night of
dwarf shrub
silence—

but simply
because her epiphany
came from
an unlicensed tabloid
psychologist
who peddles failed
weight loss
potions.

I know now
we've gone too far.
These dunes
a desert mirage

warmth
mere Ice Age relic
so I tell it
thirty-five miles north
of us:

this place
I call
our Arctic Circle.

Then Epode:

$20 to impress a 2nd grader
So I raided her wallet before school
She noticed it was gone
She noticed me

Indelible

Evening: I loaded the soiled plates,

playing
the doting Queen or
mother—ordering them into their places,
but not until
these fingers crossed the dirtiest one,
writing my elaborate initials in script and ketchup
momentarily. My mother ever watchful
reached from behind to rinse the letters away.

Morning: I emptied the clean plates,

playing
the fickle queen or
mother—pulling their round warmth
from domestic baptismal, and
scrawling my signature in the residual suds
momentarily. Her
thirsty dish towel,
finished dusting small fingerprints from the table,
swallowed my name away.

For years: The dishes

and my mother
played their game,
a Cartesian vortex of serving and being served,
washing and being washed,
and the mahogany table, begging to be sprayed
and soothed like an aging ingénue,
dutifully
offers its marred body—
evidence that children will be censored.

But not here and now:

where I load and unload myself each night
across this paper-thin table
with my daughter
a second grader whose dyslexia
requires she practice
her letters
with the regularity of a household chore.

I make note:

Steaming
inside every letter she writes
and re-writes
is a little girl today and decades ago
refusing
to ever be erased again.

Steaming
inside every bone cold plate I bury
in the cupboard
my mother, every mother.

More than Clouds

for Jean

My mother was
like the shirtwaist trend
broomstick skirt
born mid-century.
She was raised
on Stokely's sugar peas
Campbell's soup
and butter.
She was left to cry
in her crib.
She had sisters to walk with
to the store.

She was a cheerleader
flirt exceptional
student-turned-secretary
very red heels.

She wore make-up from
sun-up to sun-down
and never a day
without
calorie guilt.
She loved husband
sons daughter house with
counters dressed
in avocado green a
toaster harvest gold.

This is what I know
about my mother who knows
even less
about her own mother—
Mary—
a cruel tongue

drank one beer each night
cleansed her skunk-sprayed skin
in a tub of milk.

Who are these women?
I only know
that I want them to be
more than clouds
over this freeway
darkening the sun but they
pitch answers
that are less answers and more
warnings to stop prying.

In my family
there are no story tellers—
my mother can't
grant the meaning
of herself
the meaning of her own mother.

I am content
to hear my own daughter
claim she knows
five hundred narratives of me.

Rising Action:

Take these diet pills
Diet Coke, she whispers
Maybe an apple if you exercise
(Like me)

I Hold My Father's Beer

I

Grainy 4x4 photos
like some prop deck of saloon cards
my mother has filed
in a yellowed Polaroid Flashgun #268 box.

Meant for automatic color-pack cameras,
this box contains the cycle of life:
film to camera, exposure to development.

Now a mini-tomb
it catalogues the slideshow
of childhood. Pinafores and matching
tights meet shiny doll babies and mini kitchens.

Snapshot.
I slide the snug-fitting lid from my cache,
inhale the scent of 1972,
split-level with two car garage,
shellacked orange linoleum,
golden shag carpet.
I meet variations of myself.

I see more clearly
the woman-my-mother who gathered these pictures,
writing in skate-looped letters
my name, the year.
It is a small alphabet to unscramble
like the life I have now.
Dusty, itchy.

II

Most shots are of my legs.
Polly Flinders, patent leathers.
Fractional,

I am out of focus, off center, back to the lens.

In one frame I hold my father's beer;
in another, a pack of Salem Lights.
Most images
are presents: Christmas, birthday, Easter
Her photo omphalos,
You grainy womb,
white-washed tomb! You speak her—

don't ever forget
most important of all
is not the person,
not even
the two-and-a-half-year-old girl,
but the package.

III

The girl is package.
Nothing inside
but the facade swing-door parlor
scripted game of cards.
She'll be stuffed back into boxes.

I grow more
comfortable in the uncertainty
of being that girl, both container and
contained. In the certainty of
dust

I crave my father's cool, wet bottle of beer
and imagine the bitter sip
going down
like
a mother's expectations.

Puzzling Things

No hatreds are so keen as those of love. —Propertius

      They called me Fats.
Older brothers
have a knack
for affectionate nicknames.
Where was my mother?

The puzzle—
build one large pyramid
with six smaller pyramids
three larger pyramids
with square bases
five slanted wedges
and a large base unit.

      She was
5'1" blonde Salem Lights
front passenger seat
woody station wagon.
Disapproval
half-turn *Heads will roll*
sip of her iced tea.
My brothers'
McDonald's straws
antennae from her French-twist
L'Oréal-bleached bun

Take three
of the six small triangular pieces
place them so each triangle
has an edge
flush
with a middle wall of the base
and their points meet
in the center.

       Watching her
toward the gas station bathroom
some alien
like an oversized insect
extrasensory powers.
No one could probe me
like she could.
No one more foreign
than she was *is.*

Place one
of the larger pyramids
point down
toward the middle of the base
in between two
of the smaller triangles.

       My favorite bathing suit
white one-piece
leaf-bejeweled red tulips
red green white
eleven-year-old body.
Sunlite Water Park
Cincinnati summer—
my mother
told me
stand by the edge of the pool
for a picture
There, now you can see
how huge
your stomach looks
in a swim suit.
Where is that picture now?

The square base
of that piece
tilts up and towards

the corners
of the base. Do the same
with the other
large pyramid pieces.

Food the only thing
I was to think about.
My job to write
grocery lists
aware of pantry inventory
my way of mattering.
The irony in it
age nine
my mother's idea of bonding
dieting contests.
Who could go the longest
without eating?
Who could lose the most?
Competitions
scales portion control dizziness—
keeping a ledger
of my weight every week.

Place one of the wedge pieces
into each corner
of the base
leaning
against the larger pieces.

Now a ledger of hate.
Writing erasing inching toward
forgiveness
turn the page to see
a tulip swimsuit.
Is this how we learn to hate?

Then place the remaining

smaller pieces
on top of
the flat triangles
of the wedges.

My brothers
Weight Gain Powder.
Serious Mass High Calorie Mix
powder magical elixir for
the football field
for weigh-ins.
Threats
everything I ingested
could be tainted
with this powder.

Which broke me like
the bumper sticker
they slapped on our car
No Fat Chicks.

Slide one wedge
pointed down
into the open space
the other wedge piece
inverted
on top of it.

Today
civil with each other
photos of our kids
lamenting our aging parents
hard to reconcile
terror lived *then*
with boredom *now.*
No longer fear them
no longer revere them:

flawed beautiful
all of us.
Is this what it means
to grow up?

This move
forms the pyramid
and
completes the puzzle.

       I write
to understand why
most of my weekends
I do puzzles
obsessively pursuing solutions—
I write
to make peace with
never enjoying
a single bite of food
since I was nine.

Take the puzzle
apart
to try it again

They called me *Fats*.

Goat Song:

My mother asks
Think you're better than me?
I've practiced answering
Who could compare?

Are You My Mother?

I drive north on the 5 Freeway pointed home like the bow of some ship perhaps an aircraft carrier like the one retired in the San Diego Bay lit up with patriotic house lights a mirror image of the sunset. As I push past San Clemente's nightfall-curtain I notice heavy machinery: a front-end loader a crane and an excavator whose long arm is lifted and frozen as if to say *look* at what's become of me after my stroke *look* at my clawed hand.

I remember the baby bird from a Beginner Book in search of his mother a sad little creature paper-stepping between columns of chaos and apathy. I realize then why such a terrible story was my favorite. Not because the hatchling found its mother, but that the iron-toothed shovel spending its days digging mindless trenches in the earth finally got to lift its head and then its arm toward the sky—becoming a suspended straw-weave womb— to offer this gift, this feathered orb of frailty, this paper and bone.

This from a Rib

The genesis
of verse and versus
Adam named the animals
Eve bit back
licked the sour apple
silencing with violence
strange partnership

like J___ and T__
could not agree
what to call
me apple of their eyes
Mary or *Candice*

hoods of shame
slung on me
their marriage nibbled
by dementia's teeth
bits of flesh
failing
falling short

Clytaemnestra's
nightmare
bearing a snake
twin fangs unravel
pulse a whip
of white noise

I turn serpent
both Candice *and* Mary
_____ neither

from my father's rib
mother's womb
I sleepwalk Dunsinane
forty-seven years

their battle
still germinates
a push
like seeds in my chest.

Climax, of Sorts:

I'm getting married
Nothing feels
As funny
As her approval

At the Cheese & Olive

They sit
corner trattoria
planning their wedding
on the table
of butcher block paper
eyes closed
humming Sinatra
she orders the broccolini
watching a dog
by the front window.

He refills
Chianti
eyes closed
arms swaying feet heavy
she speaks
with the waiter
his new apartment
the line of hungry patrons
crayons
draw stick figures
groomsmen and flower girls.

Illegible guest list
blurred by drops of red
and oil adorning
like a Renaissance chapel.

That's Amore
and he
asks her to pay the bill
next door he
gets a seat at the bar
loads up
the juke box.

She's left

staring
through the glass
magic of food warmth
discarded
paper table plans
her waxy blue
red green hopes swirl
into murals.

She exits
a row of streetlights
now solemn ushers
notice.
Shadows fall
like Birnam Wood.

In the Silence of a Drive Home

for Adam z"l and Lia

What is love
you ask while drying dishes.
    is this an act of love

there can be love
in each room of the human heart
       where years of
       sheets shambolic
       catalogue
       each touch

floors
cloudy with the dust of tiny deceits
whisper / peace
whisper / gentleness
whisper into these private demesnes:
       once there was love
       and good intentions
       and a first Christmas tree
       and second-hand grief

this sand at the bottom of the tub
       is kindness;
the fleas leaping from the couch, goodness;
screen door that slams, a challenge

even lobbing screams like cannon fodder
part-time and full:
       lamentation / today
       rearranged / tomorrow
       for an ode that is riven heart

love must be what we find in the silence
of a drive home from burying
       a friend: gone

too soon the dirt,
the shovels, thousands

these mourners who know what love is
no question at all.

Catharsis:

She'll plan the wedding:
We buy the first dress we find
I twirl in the mirror
She says *suck in your gut*

At the Cheesecake Factory

He may have wanted the steak fries, but
he definitely ordered sweet potato fries;
the server repeated it *sweet potato fries?*
and he nodded yes. But when they arrived
upright like the tentacles of a sea anemone,
that rough barnacled hull of his face sunk.

I thought he was unhappy with me—
the woman whose heart like a Spanish
doubloon he lost the rainy first of January;
me the woman who wears his grandmother's
ring sixteen years now tiny diamond specks
his lil' gramma from the Great Depression;

I'm the woman who gave him three perfect
pine timber children now standing like masts
like the server behind him who returned with
ketchup who confirmed he did in fact order
the sweet potato fries. *We don't even have
steak fries* the salt she tossed into his wound.

He straightened his back as if a captain
at the helm facing down a squall, and
confirmed for all to hear that *I did* order
the steak fries then scowled at me for
the archipelago of mistakes I make, like tonight
in this half-moon bay where I eat in silence.

Married Love, Part I

I want to love you
I want to live you
I want to leave you

a letter as reckless
as the cars
down the hill

___down the street

which cradles our house
our babies
our worries

with its back turned
where we stand
each twilight
to watch the lemon

to watch the avocado
to mourn the fig
trees
that frame
the   sprawling   vista
of the Marina

with fruit so swollen
even as we watch
they fall
they feel
they fail

so over-ripe and rotting
so rotten

that we remove our sunglasses
step inside

let it all go

empty handed we
let it
it lets us

pushes us to go

Intermission:

The batter is unstirred
Water from powder back to its box
Never go without lipstick
From a house wrecked by words

Glass Jar of Volcanic Rock from Mt. Saint Helens

a present from Uncle Harry, 1980

Ten years old
We were all figuring it out
Fifth graders
Little volcanos sitting in rows
Desks like inhales
Recess our only exhale

Ten years old
All we knew of the human heart
Could fit
In that glass jar
Of volcanic rock from an uncle
In Washington

I asked my mother
What it meant
The other girls and boys
At recess or lunch
Behind the gate by Fields Ertel Road
Frenching

She swiftly informed me
That it involved
Tongues
Not something even married people do
Her fear airtight
My questions tightly screwed shut

I once saw a photo
Gutierrez' shot of the Chaitén Volcano
Pride of Chile
Neon veins lightning dirty thunder
From the caldera
Ashen plume eruption

Perfect metaphor
To prepare my own daughter
Ten years old
Collision of rock ash ice
Endless bloom of electric illumination
I tell her *unscrew the lid*

Eiron to Alazon:

Ancient Thespis could tell it
But for my fear
Obligation and guilt
I'd toss him my mask

Endurance

St. Francis of Assisi relinquished
his Daddy's money
to marry Lady Poverty
        and tend to lepers

Apparent enemy of the Vatican
Madame Guyon
closed out the better part of the 17th Century
in the Bastille
        scribbling letters to her lover

In a box of ice for 63 hours
the toast of Times Square
David Blaine
        was rescued with chain saws

Phillippe Petit sauntered across 1974
and the high-wire
        from Twin to Twin Tower

Vegan wunderkind Rich Roll
completed 5 Ironmans
        on 5 Hawaiian islands in 5 days

I have much more in common
lately it seems
with that guy from Kennesaw Georgia
who won the 11 lb. Carnivore Pizza Challenge
in under an hour—

I tell myself to just keep swallowing

Over Iced Tea at Ashland Hill

you explained
we are
a children's garden
like the one
we visit in Pasadena
the Huntington
Library

you were right
we are
made of

fire
here are the tunnels
soft halos of light
pulse of
shadow and heat
flame-colored
flax

earth
silhouettes
of magnetic sand
across
a landscape of pebbles
to drop
into a symphony

air
braided
with citrus and lavender
whimsical
as the topiary animals
watching us
like grandparents

water

for splashing
before disappearing
into the fog
swept

one might
stop
to wonder how
it can be
we don't know better

rewind
ours is a life
cruel experiment
of stretch and yield

marriage
a Promethean
dance
on separate continents
a presentation

mine
a sleeping dog
whimpering itself awake
wait

do not
confuse this field trip
ice rattling glass bottom
trip for love
that is another
type
of garden

The Chorus:

i am so embarrassed by u
all ur family is
ASHAMED
(Caps hers)

Leaving

The hours expire
find themselves fastening the buttons
of my blouse
in a strange hotel room—
assist the October night
weaving its gold and russet threads
about my neck.

This electric blue body exits
folding past itself
like the Pacific's winter tongue.

Of Your Flesh

When a glass of ice water
is more love than mother's eyes/cold as Taiz
she who has become ruffled
shadow-pattern slipping around corners and hallways

Who's there?
Is that you? Don't take the child:

       The airport's noise tonight like
distant roars (some final curse) from lions
left to starve in Yemenite zoos,
fresh complement to the rain

tonight's rain which mimics
my lifetime of heart beats
now puddling by the sliding/glass/door
as if to caution ghosts are gathering

ghosts are being released.

Can you accommodate us?
We can sleep on closet floors   or a single eyelash.
Our touch like urushiol rash.

      Mother wrote her letter
but circumcised the bottom third: scissor/frenzy
inflection before
mailing. Just so

I know she wants to say more
             You/rotten/child/insultme/goodbye
_____ A lot more. Maybe that's why

I use my own teeth (nervous habit)
to open this tongue,
the red release so nice so warm across the bone
an ivory birth

sliding/slipping
a series of drops from the rabbit's ear
into my own magician's hat.

An Episode:

Lunch alone we get to talk
What did he do to you
I cry tell her everything—
Oh is that all

Married Love, Part II

I want to
write a letter
as reckless as
the cars
metal rip tides
speeding
over our hill

this Dog Town street

I want
to write our house
watching fig
lemon and avocado
trees frame
a sprawling vista
the Marina
fruit
so swollen
they fall

overripe and rotting

I can't
write back steps
we climb
one last time
taking
off sunglasses
back inside
letting it
all drop
empty handed we
let go

only the Jacaranda knows

Opposite of the Stockholm Syndrome

What does it matter
what is between a mother and a daughter

The muskrats
and the wombats

skulking slender loris preening
in the lowlands
of our leafy reformatory?

Parenting
is a prison:

you've got the memories
in your hand

the holidays

the shiny skeleton keys.

Can you mother
me and toss
me crumbs of life
crumbs of light?

That is what it is between mother and daughter

until we are not speaking
we never spoke

all along,

my hair is growing back
appetite coming back.

You will grow
older and I will
not be there to hate it.

Happy Hour:

A glass of McCallan's
My secret
Friends don't know
I'm a *terrible daughter*

Second Language

A friend beams to me
about the ASL class she'll take this spring
and I feign delight
while swallowing the secret

that my parents taught me
sign language early:
I became fluent in their dialect
of disapproval and blistering
syntax of spite.

My friend will learn
the international sign for Happy Birthday
a grimace for *that tastes funny*
maybe a full body expression of jubilation;

I was raised to read impatience
in a double finger snap
gnarled lips of disgust
and the finger wag *shame on you.*

Perhaps she'll stumble
through the first conversations,
get tutors for finger spelling, or join
a study group to increase speed.

I was an apt student
enrolled in the total immersion program
though some signs I never learned:
I *am* enough.

Mise en Place

A married couple sits on the porch
and hear someone knocking
at the door. It is quite loud.

The wife says
Maybe we should answer
the door. It is getting louder.

Their sons are sitting in a dorm room
and also hear someone knocking
at the door. It is slow and heavy.

The older brother says
We should take care
of that constant knocking at our door.
It has become unbearable.

Years go by.

The younger brother knows the knocking
at the door is what destroyed their family.

He decides to say
Has anyone asked our sister if
she'd like to come inside?

After a few decades of listening to the knocking
at the door, the brothers become too busy to notice.

The parents become hard of hearing.

Narcissus to Echo:

"All of life, all history
happens in the body. I am
learning about the woman who carried me
inside of hers."

~ Sidda Walker, *Divine Secrets
of the Ya-Ya Sisterhood*

One for the Money

After the money comes the show,
then I get ready to go.
Is sleep another childhood?
I wonder.
Can we play in the midst of a war?

I am playing with you, Father; here
on this swinging stage, this
show-time dream. Whistle-lipped—
these hands let me go
even though I am not ready.

*

The blockage begins small, a coin
stuck in the slot. It is alone. It goes fetal
until more failures drop in,
money falling from hungry hands. And
here my purpose is formed.
Determined, as a wall of kudzu, hands clenched,
moon-face show through the curtain,
a tiny girl ready
to go deep into the beating machine,
my father's fleshy djembe.

*

My mother cooks dry pork chops
and green beans, all she can muster up. I
tear large sheets of foil; she compliments my work.
We stretch and tear the cellophane
membrane of each pink rectangular organ,
marveling at the white layer
icing of pig fat. "Help me make 'em sizzle,"
she says with a giggle. I can't look
away from the boiling potatoes.

*

I drive my father's car to his pre-op appointment—
forty-five minutes of highway trimmed
by corn and sycamore. The green
seems a playground, endless room to run or skip,
with couch cushion clouds of blue. Sky
and grass merge like *haibun*, and
I want to write calligraphy with my car. I
am ready for this show.

*

His body opens. The machine breathes for him—
one breath becomes two,
then three. At four the doctor goes.
The bloody organ offers
its plastic wrapping like a calf to the gods,
and I imagine it all. But
here in the darkness of the waiting room
I linger, I remain. Fluid.

The clock ticks like
an overbearing coach who expects too much,
and my hands tap my belly
remembering
how he gripped my ankle and wrist
swinging me out and back over my bed each night
like a heartbeat.
He stopped. I am called inside from the swings
                                        to go.

Daughter's First Facial

for Georgia

She is still
her eyes covered
crescent-shaped
her little belly
rises falls
breathes small room air

Uneasy
what to expect
next the clay-red blanket
like an arroyo
to her jackrabbit body
fingers
stroking squid tentacles
across her cheek

This woman in white
pumping lotion
in the steam
and ocean sounds
like mid-century coastal
towns French Tudor
wide-hipped roofs
I squeeze her feet

Dusk
inches from me as I sit
adult chaperone
makeshift midwife

Queen Mab
tip-toeing over my nose
I too lay prostrate
belly big as hills
West Hollywood

hospital
the dance of delivery
fourteen years ago

The white coat
coached me
pump *push* plush
warmth against my hips
churning
river delta insides
steaming milk pressing
full
force focus
on the table where
she may some day
surrender
hips wide shivering
light shining steel
plunging
her tropical island
innocence in stirrups

I will be
in that room too
at her feet

They begin to twitch
she's bored
and has no answer
to the question
about her skin regimen
when

Wrapped in wetness
and warmth
this world where
we are toweled

cheek to crown
on tables
from birth to death
cold slab
that cannot host the love
the width of a life

I cannot pull her back in
she won't be able to pull
me back
someday stiff
clay cold mask of death
peeling off
this earth-private
session now finished
cool water cup in the light.

Echo to Narcissus:

Let these words
Tiny feet padding along
Forgive
My [mother's] tenement heart

Pipe Dream

My left artery tore
spontaneously—
it's called a dissection
cardiac arrest ICU
puzzled cardiologist with
me 39 vegan fit
and yet.

I explained it
afflicted
for decades now
inflicted
upon myself
in-patient out-patient
bulimic episodes
night terrors
to round out the depression.

She told me
never *never* do it again
my heart
had had enough.
I nodded obediently while
to myself
I laughed and she scheduled
the metal stent
tiny life preserver
I float with still.

Tonight I stand
in front of
the bathroom mirror
again *again*
gray sweats and white tank
I pull my hair back
habit
to begin

dissecting the anxiety
and fear
scarfed down just
this Christmas.

I stare and wonder
will I ever stop
purging the identity
fed to me
could I ever climb back in
find my way
clawing
crawling on hands and knees
into her womb
fleshy lighthouse
low tide smuggler's cave
where
sound was muffled and I
could not yet hear
the word *fat.*

Mother of Monsters

I am half woman
half snake she-viper
an echidna
of Greek myth
a forgotten puggle
newborn
like a German
butterball potato
or a poem
little echidna
strength to demolish
whole cities
and yet
gentle pacifist
spiny tongued
muddle
feet backward
in eternal retreat
claws like reticella cuffs
avant-garde hair
forest of quills
twin female channels
heroic couplets
punctured
like a Spanish
doubloon

today
I cradle myself
echidna babe
petite puggle
stanza and then I
return
to her woodland breast
push and burrow
into her crevasse
and become

what I will become
tomorrow
half woman half snake
she-viper and
mother of monsters

Facebook:

Please don't argue on FB
I'll do what I like
Who do you think you are?
I am still. Pushing.

Mirror or Lamp

She would never admit
there was something terribly wrong
as I emerged from her
ivory womb.
My face was not
the face she remembered
sculpting

Too many days squandered
searching
the missing features—
eyes the color of home
hair that behaves
nose cute as a summer breeze
no chiseled marble
swept from Pygmalion's studio

Until reading
Galatea
whose story is therapist

a mother is not a door—
she is a security check point
where I present
my papers
my reason for being
where I sweat
the seconds the months until
the boom slowly lifts
in full salute
approval

I also know a mother is not a mirror.

That's most important
as I glance
through my daughter's Instagram

sculptor crafting her own
digital mythology
I wonder does she wish I were
a door or even a gate—
her face
so indistinguishable from mine.

I'd Take Your Hand

if you'd let me.
Make you stop already.

Then it could be my turn
with the red pencil—
its bleeding,
smearing such wicked precision.

I too am a cruel editor,
Mother.

Maybe I'd begin
on the glossy page
of *your* face,
slashing key features,
or I'd scribble No in the margin
of your body.

The sinews of my arm
buckling
like sidewalks
until I work my way
toward your neck where

…where I would circle
again and again,
tighter and tighter,
no more red to give.

So you can understand
how I live.

Texts:

A mother's words
You're done w this family
I block her
Still she pushes.

Witch Doctor

Hong Kong, 1976

My mother took us to find
a cure for my brothers' foot worm
and my fear of kindergarten
the witch doctor asked me to stand

I stared out his office window
imagined my fingers in Kowloon Bay
my six-year-old body thundering
off from Kai Tak Airport—

My mother smiled at the old man
his eyes rolled back like mahjong dice
invocation to the spirits perhaps
while my two brothers sat

comfortable refuge of twin symmetry
a catch of duck feathers now
in her hands my mother was satisfied
she placed one feather under each

of our pillows finger-soft evening
my brothers dreamt of catching snakes
I made my dolls—Southeast Asian
gifts from my father's trips—

I made them stand against the wall
of my room while I traced their shapes
with the feather wondering if I rolled
my eyes could I be important too?

Alzheimer's

for my father

The disease of a good man
who earned medals
U.S.N.A. '61
distinguished service
                        bravery

A disease of mistakes
of seclusion
eyes unfocused
names flaking away
                        erosion

This disease an eighteen-wheeler
plunging through
night fog
bake-kujira road
                        silence

It is my brothers' fear
my mother's daily brawl
my receipt
for life's sad purchase
                        madness

His own personal opera house
singing arias
mindless as Nietzsche in Basel
punching holes in the clouds
                        God

He becomes his slippers
padding measured
unmarked trail
veering from the curb
                        loose

Alzheimer's meets him
with an armadillo chest
and the wolf's velvet breath
for the halving of his
                    mind

Exode:

"Ain't nothing in the world worse
than looking at your children drowning
scared if you get to trying to save them
they might see you can't swim either."

~ Kiese Laymon, *Heavy*

The Little Miami River

is my father
filling his shirts
and slippers
with the applause
of pulses sipping
mudbank coffee
with the precision
of turnpike truckers
dabbling ducks
sliding his rook
down the tiled path
of black and white
whistling chess drunk
painting our canoe
camouflage in
the garage but first
wiping its dust
with a cheesecloth
tossing over the 80 oz.
popcorn bash-bags
like an angler
braving the summer
Southwestern Ohio
roller coaster
of typhoon peaks
and whirls only
to placate the heart
of his little girl
before silt-slow and
damned to age
or emptied tumbling
into the rapids
of dementia's big
river mouth
while I am distracted
by the shimmer
and feather of hooks

...And It's Not Me

She asks again
Who my favorite is
Come on
She pushes me
Which of the three
Do I love most
An inquiry like a swarm
Of ocean gowns

I wonder how could
A mother prefer one
Over the others
I think of my boy
My two girls
For whom I prayed
Sacred call button
To God secretly
Knitting in my womb

Each tender crown
First, second, and third
Pushing through me
Like my answer
To her secret question
Still I am pushing
Like life's first breath:
She asks for my favorite
Because she has hers

Epilogue:

Although they wear masks
Their dance is expressive
Conveyed by hands arms
And body.

Blind Man's Bluff

for daughters who learn to see themselves

a canvas wet with oils, a farm scene
in Aunt Bezzy's makeshift studio—

the easel seemed a wooden horse, her
painting dressed to ride. I was enamored.

My mother thought her sister's art silly;
how very well I knew this label *silly.*

So I picked up a round-tipped brush
and dragged it across the palette, through

puddles of mud-ochre, jade, and cerise
like I had been dragged around since

birth by my mother. Indignant, I added
my own lash of black to her red peonies.

Down the hall nothing had changed:
the cousins still giggled, prank-calling,

truth-or-daring. Yet I slid tall, now
new from under the heavy tarp of doubt.

Suddenly, the air in her studio seemed
even sweeter than my father's laughter,

sweeter than my desire to become
color living between line and shadow.

I began shedding ghosts like stories
while the smiling corner spray of sunlight

and dust became a bone-beveled frame.
When the paint dried, I swore I saw

the line-sketched face of a girl playing
Blind Man's Bluff—moments after

removing her blindfold, switching on
the light and finding a pen to *push*.

Literary Acknowledgements

"Still I am Pushing" appears as "Snow Tubing" in *The Light Ekphrastic*

"Small Places I've Filled" appears in the July issue of *The Broadkill Review*

"She Calls" appears in *White Wall Review*

"Gunkholing" appears in *LEVELER*

"Fearless Girl" appears in *Helen Literary Magazine's IMPACT: An Anthology of Social Justice*

"Daughter's Lament" appears in the fall 2017 issue of *Heavy Feather Review*

"Toward an Arctic Circle" appears in *Tiny Seed Literary Journal*

"Indelible" appears in *The Showbear Family Circus*

"More than Clouds" appears in *Dovecote Magazine*

"I Hold My Father's Beer" appears in *Cosumnes River Journal*

A non-fiction version of "Puzzling Things" appears in *Atlas and Alice*

"Glass Jar of Volcanic Rock from Mt. Saint Helens" appears in *Gyroscope Review*

"Of Your Flesh" appears in *Heartwood Literary Magazine*

"Mise en Place" appears in *Poetry Breakfast*

"One for the Money" appears in *That Literary Review*

"Pipe Dream" appears in *Cortland Review*

"Leaving" appears in *Poetry Quarterly* (titled as "Departure")

"The Little Miami River" appears in the July issue of *The Broadkill Review*

"...And It's Not Me" appears in *Heavy Feather Review*

Personal Acknowledgements

We call him *Stray Dog*, sometimes *Boss*—his name is Kevin Kelsey, and I am so grateful he is my husband. From reading drafts of poems to celebrating publications, he has always been faithful in validating my identity as a writer. And loving me. No one makes me laugh like he does. For that alone, I thank him.

Huge thanks to my daughter, Georgia, who tolerates and somehow loves me. Her free spirit and tender heart inspire me daily. Also to my son, Mikey, who teaches me how to be a better mom and amazes me with his passion for others. And to my youngest daughter, Marlene, whose creative mind and unwavering joy for life never fail to startle me.

Endless gratitude and love to my dear friends and mentors, Sheryl J. Anderson and Sara Parrott, whose insightful notes saved my work time and again. Thank you to my cousin, Tammy Klinikowski, for walking beside me through a difficult couple of years. I count her presence a great boon in my life. And much appreciation to my fellow *Daughters* Facebook group whose wisdom offers much clarity and comfort.

Finally, thank you to my teaching community of colleagues, students, and parents past and present. I could not have the confidence to write without your overwhelming support and encouragement. A special thank you to Jordy, Natalie, the faculty lounge crew, and the fabulous YULA girls' class of 2020 for celebrating this book's publication acceptance while on a loud, crowded bus back to our Ojai camp site!

CANDICE KELSEY has been researching and writing, both creatively and academically, for decades. She holds her B.A. (Miami University) and M.A. (LMU) in literature and is inspired by Nelly Sachs, Linda Pastan, Zora Neale Hurston, Herman Melville, and David Sedaris. Candice teaches English at a private Yeshiva girls' high school in Los Angeles, where she has been inspired to write her blog *Don't Nachas 'til You Try Us*. Her first book explored adolescent identity in the age of social media and was recognized as an Amazon.com Top Ten Parenting Book in 2007.

Her poetry has appeared in *Poet Lore, The Cortland Review, North Dakota Quarterly* and many other journals. She feels honored that her poem "The Birth of President Trump" was included in Sibling Rivalry Press' special issue *If You Can Hear This: Poems in Protest of an American Inauguration*. A finalist for Poetry Quarterly's Rebecca Lard Award and recipient of honorable mention in *Common Ground Review's* 2019 poetry contest, Candice's creative nonfiction was nominated for a 2019 Pushcart Prize.

Candice is the co-founder of a private high school, has served as an essay evaluator for the College Board and the U.S. Department of Education, volunteered as a fiction reader for *The New England Review*, and continues to foster a love of writing in today's youth. She is an unabashed fan of *Murder, She Wrote, Columbo*, and *The Nancy Drew Hardy Boys Mysteries* as well as all things opera and musical theater. She and her family are passionate advocates for both animal rights and foster youth. You can find her @CandiceKelsey1 @BooksBoxers and @HardyTonight as well as www.christianenglishteacheratorthodoxjewishgirlsschool.com

www.ingramcontent.com/pod-product-compliance
Lightning Source LLC
Chambersburg PA
CBHW021148090426
42740CB00008B/1004